MUDFLOWS AND LANDSLIDES

MICHAEL WOODS AND MARY B. WOODS

LERNER PUBLICATIONS COMPANY
MINNEAPOLIS

To Cathleen Woods

Editor's note: Determining the exact death toll following disasters is often difficult—if not impossible—especially in the case of disasters that took place long ago. The authors and the editors in this series have used their best judgment in determining which figures to include.

Text copyright © 2007 by Michael Woods and Mary B. Woods

Lerner Publications Company
A division of Lerner Publishing Group
241 First Avenue North
Minneapolis, MN 55401 U.S.A.

Website address: www.lernerbooks.com

Library of Congress Cataloging-in-Publication Data

Woods, Michael, 1946–
    Mudflows and landslides / by Michael Woods and Mary B. Woods.
        p.   cm. — (Disasters up close)
    Includes bibliographical references and index.
    ISBN-13: 978–0–8225–6574–1 (lib. bdg. : alk. paper)
    1. Mudflows—Juvenile literature. 2. Landslides—Juvenile literature. I. Woods,
Mary B. (Mary Boyle), 1946– II. Title.
    QE599.A2.W66 2007
    551.3'07—dc22   2006030162

Manufactured in the United States of America
1 2 3 4 5 6 – DP – 12 11 10 09 08 07

Contents

Introduction

WEIRD NOISES WOKE JUAN TACAXOY. IT WAS OCTOBER 5, 2005. TACAXOY LIVED IN PANABAJ, A VILLAGE IN THE CENTRAL AMERICAN COUNTRY OF GUATEMALA.

Mud and debris fill the area where the Guatemalan villages of Zanchaj and Panabaj used to be. Heavy rains from Hurricane Stan caused mudflows throughout Central America in October 2005.

Tacaxoy went outside and saw a 6-foot (2-meters) deep river of mud flowing toward his home. "About 10 minutes later came the water and sand," Tacaxoy said, "and a little later the rocks and tree trunks."

Tacaxoy and all 30 members of his family lived through the mudflow. Other people in Central America and southern Mexico were not so lucky. Mudflows were happening all over this area. And mud was swallowing people alive. "The problem was it was in the middle of the night, everyone was sleeping," said Dr. Francisco Mendes Beauc, who had come from a nearby village to help the survivors.

Four days of heavy rain from Hurricane Stan had soaked the ground. Rain had turned the soil into thick mud. Sheets of mud on the sides of mountains and hills began to flow downward. Rivers of mud up to 40 feet (12 m) thick poured over houses and other buildings.

Mud is heavy enough to crush buildings and carry away cars. Mud just a few inches (centimeters) deep can trap people. People buried under mud may suffocate (die from lack of air to breathe). People also may get sick from swallowing mud and breathing it into their noses.

As the mud flowed over the ground, it picked up tree branches, broken glass, and rocks the size of basketballs. Those objects scraped against people, animals, and buildings.

Alexander Flores's home in San Salvador, the capital of El Salvador, was buried under 6 feet (2 m) of mud. His mom and five of his brothers and sisters died. "I just heard two shouts from my mother, saying 'Alex, Alex,' maybe for me to help her or her trying to save me."

Deep mud covered roads and made it hard for rescue workers to arrive and help. In Panabaj, mud covered the roofs of buildings. Rescue workers could not even find homes where people might be buried.

"We are asking that [Panabaj] be declared a cemetery," said Diego Esquina, the mayor of Panabaj. "We are tired, [and] we no longer know where to dig." He said that 1,000 to 1,500 people were probably buried under the mud.

Nobody knows how many people died after Hurricane Stan because many bodies could not be found. The mudflows killed at least 750 people, injured hundreds of others, and destroyed about 100,000 people's homes.

El Salvador also experienced Hurricane Stan. That same week, the volcano Ilamatepec erupted and sent streams of hot mud, called lahars, down the mountain.

"I was like a worm sliding around in the mud."

—Alexander Flores, whose home in El Salvador was buried by a mudflow in 2005

What Are Mudflows and Landslides?

MUDFLOWS ARE WET EARTH THAT FLOWS DOWN THE SIDES OF MOUNTAINS OR HILLS. THE MUD IS THICK, ALMOST LIKE TOOTHPASTE. IT IS MADE UP OF SOIL, STONES, AND OTHER MATERIAL MIXED WITH WATER FROM RAIN OR MELTED SNOW.

Mudflows may be more than 700 feet (200 m) wide and 30 feet (9 m) deep. Some whoosh along at more than 30 miles (48 kilometers) per hour. They can go great distances. In 1877 a mudflow in Ecuador traveled more than 192 miles (309 km).

A mudflow usually gets bigger as it moves along. The flow grows by scooping up trees, soil, and rocks. Mudflows can carry away people, animals, houses, cars, bridges, and other things in their path.

LANDSLIDES

Landslides are masses of soil and rock that break loose from hills and mountains and slide down. Some landslides involve only a few rocks. In others, the whole side of a

FAST FACT: SLUMPS

Slumps *(below)* are landslides with nowhere to go. In a slump, a large amount of soil, rock, or other material drops downward. But it moves only a short distance, then piles up and stops. Slumps happen when material drops onto flat land, rather than a hillside.

In 2006 a landslide ripped apart this hillside in the Philippines.

mountain breaks off. As the dirt and rocks tumble down, they destroy anything in their way. Landslides can smash buildings like potato chips.

The material in a landslide may be wet, but it does not become a thick liquid. Landslides usually do not travel far. A landslide may move only 100 to 200 feet (30–60 m).

Landslides may happen suddenly, killing people and destroying property without warning. Others happen very slowly. Part of a hill may slip only 1 inch (2.5 centimeters) in 100 years.

A covered road is being built to protect drivers from the frequent landslides in this part of northern Italy.

ONE DISASTER LEADS TO ANOTHER

Mudflows and landslides can cause terrible disasters. Disasters are events involving great destruction. Mudflows and landslides damage buildings, underground pipes, electric wires, and other property.

Each year in the United States, mudflows and landslides kill 25 to 50

CREEPY GRAVESTONES

Have you ever seen old gravestones in a cemetery? Did any of them lean downhill? If so, creep probably tilted them. Creep is a very slow movement of the ground. The soil may move only 0.1 inch (0.25 cm) each year. Although it takes many years, creep can tilt gravestones, fences, trees, and other objects in the ground.

Heavy rains loosened a cemetery-packed hillside above the town of Teziutlán in south central Mexico. The massive mudflow in 1999 buried as many as 200 people.

people. They injure hundreds of people and cause up to $2 billion in damage. In the rest of the world, these disasters may cause thousands of deaths and injuries each year. They may cause many billions of dollars in damage.

Mudflows and landslides can set the stage for other disasters. Landslides that block rivers can cause floods. Landslides on the ocean floor can cause tsunamis. These monster waves can crash down on the shore, causing great damage. In 1998 an undersea landslide caused a tsunami that killed thousands of people in Papua New Guinea.

In 1998 a tsunami destroyed several villages in northern Papua New Guinea.

In California's Sierra Nevada range, a landslide fans out toward Lake Tahoe. The massive landslide closed Highway 89 for 18 months.

Scientists removed the mud that buried the Roman town of Herculaneum nearly 2,000 years ago.

A.D. 79
HERCULANEUM

About 5,000 people lived in Herculaneum. That beautiful seaside town was in the modern country of Italy. People went there to escape the hot, noisy cities. They enjoyed the bright sun and blue water of the Bay of Naples.

Herculaneum is located at the foot of Mount Vesuvius. This mountain is a volcano—an opening in Earth's surface that sometimes erupts. During an eruption, smoke, ash (tiny bits of rock), and hot gases come out of the volcano. Melted rock and mud also may flow down the volcano's sides.

On August 24, A.D. 79, Mount Vesuvius erupted. This eruption is famous for burying the nearby city of Pompeii in ash. It also buried Herculaneum in mud. Steam (water in the form of a hot gas) or liquid water was released during the eruption. It mixed with black, sandy ash deposited on Vesuvius's sides during earlier eruptions and became mud.

A student named Pliny the Younger watched the eruption. He was staying with his mother and his uncle about 20 miles (32 km) away, in the town of Misenum.

"[A] fearful black cloud . . . parted to reveal great tongues of fire . . . ," Pliny wrote. **"[D]arkness fell . . . as if the lamp had been put out in a closed room."**

Vesuvius began to erupt shortly after noon. At first people in Herculaneum probably just stayed put. By late afternoon, the eruption got worse. People probably started to flee.

Nobody knows what it was like in Herculaneum as people tried to escape from the disaster. Pliny saw terrible scenes nearby in Misenum. **"[S]ome were calling their parents,"** he wrote, **"others their children or their wives. . . . [S]ome . . . prayed for death in their terror of dying."**

It may have been hard for people to escape from Herculaneum. Mud often flows faster than people can run. It may flow as fast as 33 miles per hour (53 km/hr). Herculaneum was buried under mud up to 75 feet (23 m) thick. The town remained lost to the world for almost 1,800 years. In 1709 people digging a well

> **You could hear the *shrieks* of women, the wailing of infants, and the shouting of men.**
>
> —Pliny the Younger, who witnessed the eruption of Italy's Mount Vesuvius in A.D. 79

rediscovered it. We know that at least 332 people died in the mudflow. Scientists have found those bodies preserved in the hardened mud.

Mud coated buildings, statues, tools, and other things in the town. The mud preserved these objects. When scientists removed the mud, they saw what life was like 2,000 years ago.

Archaeologists have uncovered human skeletons in Herculaneum. The volcanic mudflow killed residents instantly.

What Causes Mudflows and Landslides?

MUDFLOWS AND LANDSLIDES BOTH HAPPEN BECAUSE OF A FORCE—SOMETHING THAT PUSHES OR PULLS ON OBJECTS. THAT FORCE IS GRAVITY. GRAVITY PULLS OBJECTS TOWARD EARTH'S CENTER. IT HOLDS DISHES ON THE TABLE. IT KEEPS PEOPLE FROM FLOATING IN THE AIR.

In the same way, gravity pulls on rocks and soil on the sides of hills or mountains. Those objects usually don't tumble down because they have inertia. Inertia makes still objects stay still. And it makes objects in motion stay in motion.

Rocks and soil also stay in place because of friction. Friction is a force that makes it harder for one object to slide against another. Gravity alone isn't strong enough to overcome friction and make objects move. Gravity needs a helping hand.

GIVING GRAVITY A HAND

Rain or melting snow often lends a hand. Water soaking into soil makes the soil heavier. About 2 inches (5 cm) of rain adds almost 50,000 pounds (23,000 kilograms) of water to a 50-by-100-foot (15 m by 31 m) area of soil.

HEAVY MUD

Mud can suck the shoes and socks off your feet because it is so heavy. Just 1 gallon (4 liters) of water weighs about 8.3 pounds (3.6 kg). Mud can be more than twice as heavy as water. That's because it is water plus dirt and stones. That weight crushes buildings caught in mudflows. It also presses on people and makes it difficult for them to escape.

In Indonesia, homeowners try to move through heavy mud following a mudflow in 2006.

"After four or five days [of rain], you could have 125 tons [113 metric tons] of water, and that water's got to go somewhere," said Tom Horning, a geologist. Water helps soil overcome friction and become slippery. Water-soaked soil can slide more easily than dry soil.

Certain kinds of soil and rock slip easily. Loose soil that lies on top of solid rock is very dangerous. Rain can soak the soil, but it cannot drain away through the rock. The soil gets heavier and heavier. Just as water on a floor can make a person slip, water can make the soil slip over the underlying rock.

Loose clay is dangerous too. In 1971 heavy rain soaked a layer of loose clay and sand around the village of Saint-Jean-Vianney in Quebec, Canada. A river of mud flowed into the village. It buried 31 people and destroyed 40 homes.

DID YOU KNOW?

Geologists are the scientists who study mudflows and landslides. Geologists study how Earth formed, what our planet is like, and how it is changing. Geology is one of the earth sciences, or geosciences, that include everything about planet Earth.

ONE DISASTER LEADS TO ANOTHER

Other kinds of disasters often cause mudflows and landslides. Those disasters include hurricanes, earthquakes, and volcanic eruptions.

Hurricanes are huge storms that produce heavy rain. The rain soaks the ground and may cause mudflows.

Earthquakes are shaking movements of the ground. Earthquakes can cause landslides. When the ground shakes, loose rocks and soil on top of hills and mountains can tumble down, like popcorn falling from a shaken bowl. In 2005 a strong earthquake in Pakistan, a country in southern Asia, caused landslides that killed hundreds of people. "Whole mountainsides have disappeared," said Rab Nawaz, who was in Pakistan at the time.

A massive earthquake in Pakistan in 2005 caused aftershocks and landslides that killed many people and destroyed many roads such as this one.

"There is just a big gap where the mountain has slipped into the river."

Volcanoes have caused some of the world's worst mudflows. Soil on the slopes of a volcano is made from volcanic ash and dust. This soil is very fine. When it mixes with water, the soil changes into slippery mud. The mud can flow quickly down the mountain's sides. Volcanic mudflows are called lahars.

Volcanoes supply the water that causes lahars. Heat from an eruption can melt snow and ice on the sides of a volcano. An eruption also may release steam or underground pools of water.

Mudflows from volcanic eruptions may be boiling hot. They can burn people and animals to death. In 1985 more than 23,000 people died in the hot mud flowing from a volcano in the South American country of Colombia.

PEOPLE PLAY A ROLE

Some things that people do can cause mudflows and landslides. People's actions also can make these disasters worse.

Some mudflows and landslides happen because of deforestation (the clearing of trees). People cut down too many trees and other plants on mountains and hillsides. Plants have roots that grow down into the soil. The roots help to hold the soil in place. The leaves and branches of plants also slow down

Deforestation led to this mudflow in Japan.

In 1982 a lahar flowed down the sides
of Galunggung, a volcano on the island
of Java in Indonesia.

rain as it falls. They act like umbrellas. They keep rain from splashing onto the soil and washing it away.

Bare mountainsides and hillsides are disasters waiting to happen. People living in villages around Mount Sarno in Italy cut trees on the mountainside. They cleared bushes and grass to make fields for farming. In 1998 heavy rains sent rivers of mud roaring down the bare ground. The mudflows killed about 135 people.

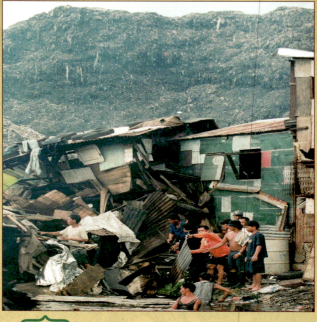

In 2000, a tall, unstable pile of garbage mixed with rain fell on the makeshift housing of residents in Quezon City, a suburb of Manila, in the Philippines.

GARBAGE SLIDE!

Things that people build also can cause landslides. For years, the city of Manila, in the Philippines in southeastern Asia, dumped its garbage in one spot. The pile of garbage grew into a mountain 70 feet (20 m) high. Hundreds of poor people lived around the pile. They earned money by sorting through the garbage and selling trash that could be recycled.

In July 2000, heavy rain soaked the garbage with water. Part of the mountain of trash slid down. "I was sleeping when I thought I heard an airplane coming," said nine-year-old Nelda Taglo. "Then there was an explosion. My papa saved me." The garbage slide killed at least 200 people. Piles of sand, coal, and other material can slide in the same way.

Houses, roads, and other structures built in the wrong places also can cause landslides. Soil has to be moved to build these structures. Hills may end up steeper than they were before. Then the ground is more likely to slip. The weight of these structures also can cause soil and rock to tumble down.

"*It's the fault of all of us,* because we destroyed nature, we *burned forests* to build houses."

—Francesco Amato, who carried his family to safety after a mudflow hit Sarno, Italy, in 1998.

The northeastern face of Turtle Mountain broke off in 1903, burying the people in the town of Frank.

1903
TURTLE MOUNTAIN

Native Americans of the Blackfoot tribe called Turtle Mountain "the mountain that moves." They knew that pieces of Turtle Mountain–located in Alberta, Canada–often tumbled down. One landslide in 1853 killed 100 Blackfoot warriors. After that, Native American people stayed away from Turtle Mountain.

Later, settlers who moved to Canada from Europe built a town called Frank right next to Turtle Mountain. About 600 people lived there. Many of them worked in coal mines–tunnels dug deep inside the mountain to get coal to burn for heat and energy.

On April 29, 1903, Turtle Mountain moved again. At 4:10 A.M., 90 million tons (82 million t) of rock and dirt broke off from the side of the mountain. The material roared down the mountainside at 85 miles per hour (140 km/hour). It rushed right into the town of Frank.

"After the mighty roar that woke me . . . a terrific weight came down on us and I could not move," said Jessie Leitch. *". . . [W]e could feel someone walking above us. . . ."*

The limestone landslide lasted only about 100 seconds. Not much remained of Frank afterward.

The landslide smashed houses and other buildings. Leitch's parents and four brothers died when their house was buried. In some spots, the rock and dirt from the landslide was more than 52 feet (16 m) deep.

As the landslide tumbled down, it shook Turtle Mountain. The coal mine's tunnels shook so hard that they caved in. Miners working in them were trapped.

The landslide buried about 1 mile (1.6 km) of tracks of the Canadian Pacific Railroad. Sid Choquette, a railroad worker, realized that a train was due to arrive in minutes. As rocks continued to fall, Choquette ran down the tracks and signaled for the train to stop. If it had crashed into the wall of rock lying on the track, many passengers would have died.

The coal mines may have weakened the mountain and helped cause the landslide. But Turtle Mountain moved long before the mines were dug. Scientists think water from rain and melting snow seeped into cracks in the mountain. The water then froze. When water freezes into ice, it expands (gets larger). The ice may have opened bigger cracks that caused the landslide that buried the town of Frank.

At least 70 people died when Turtle Mountain moved. It was the worst landslide in Canada's history.

" On a night of radiant moonlight, I had prepared for bed and went to say goodnight to my parents. I kissed them and said goodnight. I never saw them again. "

— Jessie Byran Leitch, a survivor of the 1903 Turtle Mountain landslide in Alberta, Canada

Mudflow and Landslide Country

LANDSLIDES CAN HAPPEN WHEREVER THERE ARE HIGH PLACES. THE HIGH SPOTS OFTEN ARE NATURAL FORMATIONS—MOUNTAINS, HILLS, OR CLIFFS. THEY ALSO MAY BE PILES OF SOIL, GARBAGE, OR OTHER MATERIAL BUILT BY PEOPLE.

Mudflows happen in high places where water is present. Mudflows need water to form mud. That water usually comes from rain or melting snow.

LANDSLIDE COUNTRY

Billions of people around the world live in areas affected by landslides and mudflows. Some live near steep mountains, such as Canada's Rocky Mountains.

In the United States, landslides or mudflows are common in most of the western states. They also happen in

$$$ SLIDE

The most expensive landslide in U.S. history happened in Thistle, Utah, in 1983 *(below)*. A wall of soil and rock 1,000 feet (300 m) wide, 200 feet (60 m) thick, and 1 mile (1.6 km) long blocked the Spanish Fork River. The river flooded the town of Thistle. The landslide also blocked a highway and railroad lines. It caused about $500 million in damage.

Alaska and parts of Hawaii and Puerto Rico. In the Midwest, landslide country includes the valleys of the Ohio, Missouri, and Mississippi rivers. In the East, the risk is highest in the Appalachian Mountains and in New England.

Many other landslides and mudflows happen in the Ring of Fire. That is a region surrounding the Pacific Ocean. Most of the world's volcanic eruptions and earthquakes happen there. The ring runs north from Chile along the South American and North American coasts to Alaska. It continues east to Japan and the Philippines and south to New Zealand.

Terrible mudflows have happened near volcanoes in the United States, especially Mount Rainier and Mount Saint Helens in Washington State. About 500 years ago, for example, rivers of mud 16 feet (5 m) deep flowed from Mount Rainier. Few people lived nearby when this happened. Since then, however, more people have moved to the area. About 100,000 people live right where the mud could flow.

Thousands of people would be affected if mud flowed down Mount Rainier again.

DISASTER ZONES

Mudflows and landslides happen all around the world. This map shows just a few of the major mudflow and landslide disasters that have taken place over the centuries. The boxed information describes some of the most important disasters.

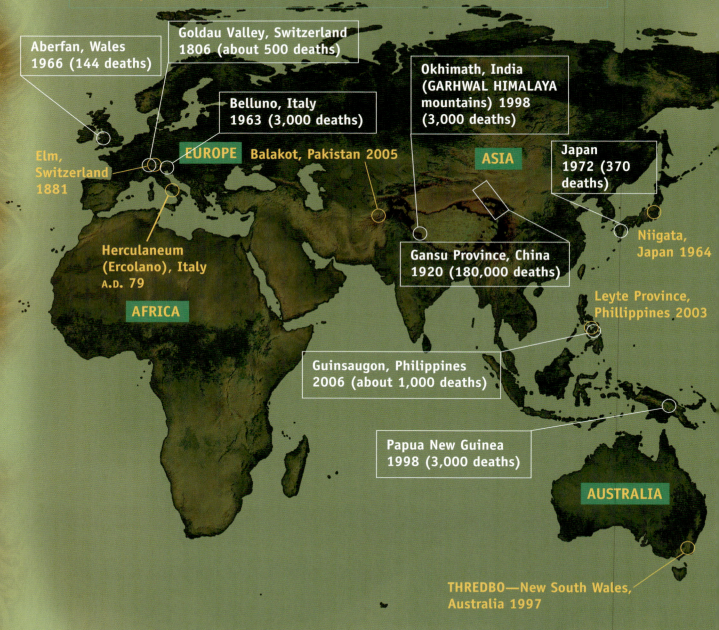

Aberfan, Wales
1966 (144 deaths)

Goldau Valley, Switzerland
1806 (about 500 deaths)

Okhimath, India
(GARHWAL HIMALAYA
mountains) 1998
(3,000 deaths)

Belluno, Italy
1963 (3,000 deaths)

Elm,
Switzerland
1881

EUROPE

Balakot, Pakistan 2005

ASIA

Japan
1972 (370
deaths)

Herculaneum
(Ercolano), Italy
A.D. 79

Niigata,
Japan 1964

AFRICA

Gansu Province, China
1920 (180,000 deaths)

Leyte Province,
Phillippines 2003

Guinsaugon, Philippines
2006 (about 1,000 deaths)

Papua New Guinea
1998 (3,000 deaths)

AUSTRALIA

THREDBO—New South Wales,
Australia 1997

TURTLE MOUNTAIN
(Alberta, Canada)
1853 (about 100 deaths)
1903 (70 deaths)

Lituya Bay, AK 1958

Saint-Jean-Vianney
(Quebec, Canada) 1971

MOUNT SAINT HELENS
—Washington 1980

NORTH AMERICA

Thistle,
Utah 1983

Haiti and the
Dominican Republic 2004

La Conchita, California 2005

Mameyes, Puerto Rico
1985 (at least 129
deaths)

Panabaj, Guatemala
2005 (750+ deaths)

Medellín, Colombia
1987 (200 deaths)

Armero, Colombia
1985 (23,000+ deaths)

COTOPAXI VOLCANO—Ecuador 1877

SOUTH AMERICA

MOUNT HUASCARÁN (Peru)
1970 (18,000 deaths)

27

1980 MOUNT SAINT HELENS

The dark part of Mount Saint Helens is where the lahar flowed during the eruption in 1980.

TV news reporter Dave Crockett was filming a report on Mount Saint Helens, a volcano in Washington State. Suddenly, Crockett felt the ground shake. He heard a rumble. The volcano was erupting.

"I . . . looked in my rearview mirror and there was just a wall of [rock and mud]," he said. *"The whole valley was just disappearing behind me."*

Crockett almost was buried alive in the biggest landslide and mudflow ever recorded. The disaster started when hot gas from the eruption melted snow and ice on Mount Saint Helens's sides. About 46 billion gallons (174 billion l) of hot water rushed down the mountain. The water picked up soil and became a mudflow.

Janet Hicks and her husband watched from a distance as the mudflow carried houses and tractors past their home. Then a big wave of mud carried their house away. **"We were numb and scared,"** said Hicks.

At almost the same time, the eruption blew off Mount Saint Helens's top. The uppermost 1,300 feet (400 m) of the mountain tumbled down in a landslide. Dorothy and Keith Stoffel were eyewitnesses. These scientists were flying above Mount Saint Helens in an airplane. **"Within a matter of seconds, perhaps 15 seconds, the whole north side of the [top] began to move,"** said Keith Stoffel.

The landslide covered an area of 24 square miles (62 square km). It moved more than 13 miles (21 km) down the mountainside into a valley below. At one point, the landslide spilled right over a hill more than 1,150 feet (351 m) high. It filled parts of the valley to a depth of about 150 feet (46 m).

> " *I was **amazed and excited** with the realization that we were watching this landslide of **unbelievable** proportions.* "
>
> —Keith Stoffel, a scientist who witnessed the 1980 eruption of Mount Saint Helens in Washington State

Spirit Lake was in the landslide's path. The lake's water usually is cold— about 42°F (5.6°C). When the hot rock and soil fell in, the water temperature rose to 100°F (38°C). Rock and mud 300 feet (90 m) deep collected on the lake's bottom.

The mudflows and landslides carried rocks, boulders as big as cars, and whole trees. They destroyed everything in their path, including millions of trees, about 200 homes, 27 bridges, and 185 miles (298 km) of roads. The disaster killed 57 people.

Heavy ash buried this car after the volcano blew.

Measuring Mudflows and Landslides

MEASURING DISASTERS IS IMPORTANT. PEOPLE NEED TO KNOW HOW SERIOUS DISASTERS ARE. THAT INFORMATION CAN HELP RESCUE WORKERS DECIDE HOW MUCH HELP TO SEND. SCIENTISTS CAN USE THE INFORMATION TO STUDY DISASTERS. SOMETIMES SCIENTISTS LEARN LESSONS THEY CAN USE TO REDUCE THE DAMAGE FROM FUTURE DISASTERS.

Scientists have developed scales for measuring some kinds of disasters. The Saffir-Simpson scale, for instance, measures the strength of hurricanes. On this scale, a Category 4 hurricane has stronger winds and causes more damage than a Category 1 hurricane. Scientists use the landslide velocity (speed) scale to describe landslides.

PUTTING LANDSLIDES IN CLASSES

The landslide velocity scale was invented in 1996 by David J. Varnes and David M. Cruden. These geologists put landslides into different classes (groups) numbered from 1 to 7. The classes are based on the speed at which the rock and soil moves and the amount of damage that happens.

The fastest landslides are Class 7. These landslides whoosh down at more than 15 feet (5 m) per second. They can cause huge disasters. They can destroy buildings and kill many people. Class 6 landslides cause less damage than Class 7 landslides. But they still kill or injure people who do not have enough time to escape.

The slowest landslides have the lowest numbers on the scale. Class 2 landslides may tilt fences. Over time, they may crack walls or cause other

The Turtle Mountain landslide of 1903 was a Class 7 disaster.

LANDSLIDE VELOCITY SCALE

CLASS	DESCRIPTION	SPEED IN INCHES/DAY	SPEED IN CM/DAY	AMOUNT OF DAMAGE
1	EXTREMELY SLOW	< 0.0017	< 0.0043	THE MOVEMENT IS SO SLOW THAT IT CAN BE DETECTED ONLY WITH SPECIAL INSTRUMENTS.
2	VERY SLOW	0.0017–0.17	0.0043–0.43	BUILDINGS AND ROADS HAVE ONLY MINOR DAMAGE.
3	SLOW	0.17–17	0.43–43	SOME DAMAGED BUILDINGS CAN BE REPAIRED DURING THE MOVEMENT.
4	MODERATE	17–1,700	43–4,300	ROADS AND STRONG BUILDINGS CAN BE REPAIRED TEMPORARILY DURING THE MOVEMENT.
5	RAPID	1,700–170,000	4,300–430,000	PEOPLE ARE ABLE TO ESCAPE. BUILDINGS ARE DAMAGED.
6	VERY RAPID	170,000–17,000,000	430,000–43,000,00	SOME PEOPLE ARE KILLED. BUILDINGS ARE DESTROYED.
7	EXTREMELY RAPID	> 17,000,000	> 43,000,000	THIS IS A MAJOR DISASTER. PEOPLE HAVE NO TIME TO ESCAPE, SO MANY DIE. BUILDINGS ARE DESTROYED.

damage to buildings. Class 1 landslides move so slowly that they can't be seen. Scientists use instruments to measure these landslides.

DANGER SIGNS

People often see or hear warning signs before major landslides take place. Cracks may open in the ground. Telephone poles may start to lean. The warnings give people a chance to evacuate (leave for a safer place). But the landslide still may harm property.

Moderate and slow landslides don't provide as many warning signs. But these slowpokes may give people enough time to build walls or fences to protect roads or buildings in their path.

LANDSLIDES YOU'VE SEEN

Have you ever traveled along a road that runs through steep hills? If you have, did you see any rocks along the sides of the road? They probably tumbled down during small landslides. People sometimes build high wire fences along roads that are next to steep cliffs. The fences keep rocks from landing on the road and causing car accidents.

SPEED AND SIZE

Speed is very important. A mountainside that breaks off and falls in a split second probably will cause more damage than a landslide that takes weeks to happen. Fast landslides also hurt more people than slow landslides. That's because fast landslides give people little time to escape.

The seriousness of a landslide or mudflow also depends on the amount of land that moves. The 1980 landslide at Mount Saint Helens involved 3.7 billion cubic yards (2.8 billion cubic m) of soil and rock. Mount Saint Helens was a much worse disaster than a 2005 mudflow in La Conchita, California. That mudflow involved only 250,000 cubic yards (191,000 cubic m) of dirt.

WILL LAND SLIDE?

Scientists measure the risk that landslides and mudflows will happen in different places. Knowing the risk is important. If people know a landslide

In 2005, mud raced down the hillside in La Conchita, giving residents of this California town little time to escape.

or mudflow is likely, they can prepare for it. They can take steps to limit the amount of damage these events will cause.

People can avoid building homes in areas that have a high risk of landslides. People who already live in a danger zone can stay alert during rainy weather or other conditions that can cause a mudflow or landslide. If the ground begins to slide, they will have a better chance of escaping.

To measure the risk, scientists check the steepness of hills or mountains in areas where people live. They find out how much rain the area gets and the kinds of soil and rock in the ground. Scientists

QUICK CLAY SLIDES

Some places in Canada, Sweden, Norway, and other northern countries have a special kind of clay under the ground. It is called quick clay. It looks like regular clay. Smack a chunk of it, however, and it turns into muddy water. Earthquakes give quick clay that same kind of smack. When the ground shakes, the hard clay under the surface becomes mud. Then the land above the quick clay slides down.

These houses in Gothenburg, Sweden, were built on a clay bed. The clay gave way during a landslide in 1977.

A scientist in the Philippines uses a map to show where landslides are likely to happen.

also find out whether earthquakes or volcanic eruptions happen nearby and whether landslides have happened in the past.

LISTENING TO ROCKS

Small soil and rock movements often happen before bigger landslides. Scientists use instruments to measure these movements.

Scientists use devices called tiltmeters to measure changes in the tilt (steepness) of mountains and hills. Several tiltmeters may be placed in holes drilled into a mountain. The tiltmeters send signals that show any movement in the mountainside. Any change may mean a landslide is coming.

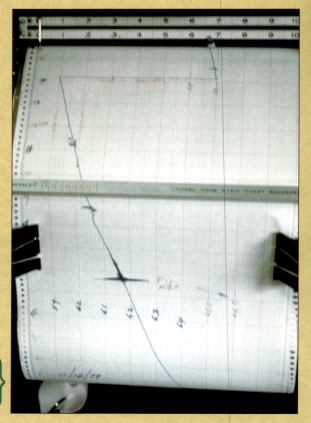

Other devices show how far the ground has moved. These devices get signals from the Global Positioning Satellite (GPS) system. Satellites are unmanned spacecraft that circle Earth. GPS satellites show the position of every point on Earth.

Scientists may also listen to rocks. They use microphone-like tools. These tools let them hear sounds that rock makes as it slides.

A tiltmeter measures movement of Hawaii's Kilauea Volcano.

A landslide took away the foundation of this house near Wellington, New Zealand, in 2006.

1985
NEVADO DEL RUIZ

After the eruption of Nevado del Ruiz, a volcano in Colombia, the mixture of ash, ice, and snow created a massive mudflow.

On November 13, 1985, geology student Jose Luis Restrepo and his friends were on a college field trip. They had traveled by bus to Armero, Colombia, a city of about 27,000 people. After going out to eat, they went back to their hotel and listened to the radio. Around 11 P.M., the radio station suddenly went off the air. A few seconds later, the electricity went off.

"[T]hat's when we started hearing the noise in the air," said Restrepo, *"like something toppling, falling. . . . Suddenly, I heard bangs, and looking towards the rear of the hotel I saw something like foam, coming down out of the darkness. . . . It was a wall of mud approaching the hotel, and sure enough, it crashed against the rear of the hotel and started crushing walls."*

Restrepo and his friends ran for their bus in the hotel parking lot. They discovered that it **"was higher than us on a wave of mud and on fire."**

The mudflow had traveled 30 miles (48 km) from the top of the Nevado del Ruiz volcano. Although Colombia's weather is very warm, Nevado del

Rescuers try to pull a body from the mud in Armero.

Ruiz is more than 17,500 feet (5,334 m) high. At its top, the air is very cold.

Snow about 30 feet (9 m) deep covered the volcano's top. The mountain also had glaciers (sheets of ice) up to 300 feet (90 m) thick. During the eruption, hot gas and melted rock poured out of Nevado del Ruiz. That hot material melted the ice and snow. The water formed one of the world's deadliest mudflows.

Mud poured down the mountain and headed toward Armero. People in the city had no warning. Many were already in bed, sound asleep.

"[The mud] dragged me about 2 miles [3 km]," said Modesto Menesses, a taxi driver in Armero. **"[It] grabbed me and pushed me under. I would come up again and again. I couldn't**

breathe....The mud was in my nose, mouth, and ears."

Alba Triviedo heard the mud's roar and took her children outside. **"The mud tore down our house,"** Triviedo said. **"Everything around us was**

> " *I covered my face, thinking, this is where I die a horrible death.* "
>
> —Jose Luis Restrepo, describing his experiences during the 1985 Nevado del Ruiz mudflow in Colombia

destroyed, but it didn't touch us. It was a miracle we lived."

About 23,000 people in Colombia—including 3 out of every 4 people in Armero—were buried alive in the mud. The mudflow injured 4,500 other people. It destroyed much of Armero and a nearby village, including the homes where 8,000 people lived. The damage totaled $1 billion.

People Helping People

PEOPLE NEED HELP AFTER A BIG MUDFLOW OR LANDSLIDE. SOME PEOPLE MAY BE TRAPPED UNDER MUD, STONES, OR THE WRECKAGE OF BROKEN BUILDINGS. OTHERS MAY HAVE CUTS OR BROKEN BONES. SOME MAY HAVE LOST THEIR HOMES. THEY MAY HAVE NO CLOTHING, WATER, OR FOOD.

Getting help to victims of mudflows or landslides can be hard. Roads often are blocked, and bridges are smashed. Rescue workers may have trouble getting in.

DIFFICULT DISASTERS

When rescue workers do arrive, their work is harder than in some other disasters. After earthquakes, for instance, victims may be trapped under broken buildings. After mudflows and landslides, people may be trapped under buildings that are covered with mud or rocks.

"You can see only the roofs of a few houses," said a rescue official at a landslide in Medellín, Colombia. The workers tried to dig through dirt 36 feet (11 m) deep with shovels, sticks, and even their bare hands.

MUDDY MYSTERY

A woman looked out her window one night in 1971 and was amazed to see lights from the next village. A hill had always blocked that view. She called a friend, and they discussed what might have happened to that hill. They didn't know that heavy rain had turned the hill into a 66-foot-high (20 m) river of mud. It was rushing toward the woman's house in Saint-Jean-Vianney, Quebec, Canada. The mudflow swept the woman away, along with a bridge, a bus, 40 houses, and 30 other people.

Rocks blocked the roads to hard-to-reach villages after an earthquake shook northern Pakistan in 2005.

Fast action is important in these disasters. People buried in mud cannot breathe. Without air, they can live for only a few minutes. But some lucky ones are buried in places where air is trapped in pockets (holes). They may live for days while waiting for help.

THE NOSE KNOWS

In poor countries, rescue workers often use poles to search for victims buried by mudflows or landslides. Workers gently push the poles into the dirt, hoping to feel when the poles touch a body. Then they move a few steps ahead and push again.

Rescue workers in richer countries have better ways of searching for victims. These workers often use rescue dogs. Dogs can smell and hear much better than people. Rescue dogs are trained to use their noses and ears to find victims. When a dog finds a person, rescue workers can dig quickly and free the person.

In the 2005 mudflow in La Conchita, California, rescuers lowered microphones into holes in the wreckage. The microphones were powerful enough to pick up moans, breathing, and other sounds made by buried people.

WHAT A RELIEF!

While rescue workers search for survivors, the other victims need relief. They need help to reduce their suffering. "What we need most is medicine, mattresses, blankets, and jackets," said Diego Esquina. He was the mayor of Panabaj, Guatemala, when it was hit by a mudflow in 2005.

CADAVER DOGS

Search and rescue teams try to find living disaster victims, but they also look for people who have died. These teams use cadaver dogs, which are trained to find the scent of cadavers (dead human bodies). Finding these bodies is very important. When a victim's body is found, the victim's family and friends can accept that the person really is dead. They can express grief over their loss and say good-bye to their loved one.

Boonie, a cadaver dog, searches for bodies following a deadly landslide in La Conchita, California, in 2005.

Medicine and household items aren't all that victims of mudflows and landslides need. Some of them may have lost everything they own. Their homes may be so badly damaged that it is unsafe to go back inside. They need a new place to live.

People often have to evacuate to another area, away from the disaster. At first, they may live in tents or in shelters. Shelters often are schools or other buildings. They have beds and food for people who have evacuated.

DISASTER RELIEF WORKERS

In the United States, the first help in a disaster usually comes from local fire departments and police. They arrive at the scene quickly and go to work. In big disasters, soldiers from the U.S. Army and the National Guard and workers from the Federal Emergency Management Agency (FEMA) also help. They provide water, food, clothing, and places for people to live. Fire and police departments from other cities also may send rescue workers.

After the La Conchita mudflow, workers from 20 different agencies went to work within minutes of the disaster. The local chapter of the American Red Cross, for instance, opened eight shelters.

People from around the country often give money to help the victims. Stores and other businesses may send water, clothing, and other products.

MANY HELPING HANDS

In other countries, some help comes from the International Federation of Red Cross and Red Crescent Societies. This is the world's biggest private organization that helps in disasters. Red Cross and Red Crescent workers stay for months to help people rebuild their lives. Almost all countries have a Red Cross or Red Crescent organization. When a disaster strikes, people from around the world help by sending money to those organizations.

The United Nations, a group of more than 190 countries, also provides relief after disasters. The governments of the United States and other countries send workers and money.

Soldiers unload relief supplies after a mudflow cut off villages in the northeastern Philippines in 2004.

DISASTER RELIEF KITS

The first help for survivors often comes in kits that relief workers pass out. Water is one of the most important items in these kits. Mudflows and landslides can break pipes that carry drinking water. They also can pollute wells, rivers, and lakes where people get water to drink.

Polluted water contains germs. If people drink it, they can get very sick. Some people who survive a disaster die because they had to drink polluted water.

Relief kits contain a few bottles of water to keep people healthy until trucks and airplanes can bring in much more. The kits also contain food, blankets, soap, and other important items.

GETTING A LIFE BACK

After the relief efforts end, disaster victims need help to recover. They need help getting their lives back to normal. Even after terrible disasters, people do spring back. They rebuild roads, bridges, and even entire cities. Schools, stores, and movie theaters open again. People go back to work and live normally.

Rebuilding lives can take a long time. That's especially true in poorer countries, where the governments cannot afford to provide much help to their people. In these countries, some of the money for rebuilding comes from the same organizations that provided disaster relief.

In the United States, many people have insurance for their homes and cars. People with insurance pay small amounts of money to insurance companies. Then, if a disaster strikes, the insurance company provides money to replace or repair damaged items.

Recovery may mean moving out of harm's way. Mudflows and landslides often happen over and over in the same areas. FEMA sometimes buys the homes of people who live in these areas. The people use the money to move to a safer place. Then they will not become disaster victims again.

In December 2004, a shopkeeper shoveled mud from the entrance to his business in Infanta, the Philippines.

> **"We have nothing left. Everything is destroyed. We didn't even manage to save our clothes."**
>
> —Celia Huerto, whose family survived a series of tropical storms and mudflows in the Philippines in 2004

A photo taken from the air shows the devastation caused by the mudflow in La Conchita.

2005
LA CONCHITA, CALIFORNIA

Rain soaked La Conchita, California. This town of 240 people had had almost as much rain in two weeks as it usually does in a year. La Conchita is located on a narrow strip of land. The Pacific Ocean is on one side. Steep hills about 600 feet (180 m) high are on the other.

People were worried about the hills. After heavy rain in 1995, the hills had slid into La Conchita, burying houses under 600,000 tons (540,000 t) of mud. *"We knew the mountain was coming down [again],"* said Greg Ray, who lived in the town. But nobody knew when.

After the 1995 mudflow, the county government put up signs outside La Conchita. They warned, "Enter at Your Own Risk." But people took the signs down. *"Everyone got used to [the risk of another mudflow],"* said Gisela Woggon, another resident. *"People started moving back, even moving into houses at the edge of the old slide."*

Around 12:30 P.M. on January 10, 2005, the hills slid into La Conchita again. Ray and his friend Tony Alvis were helping a neighbor move out of a house below a steep hill. **"[John Morgan, another neighbor,] yelled at us and said, 'The mountain's coming down—get out of there now!'"**

They ran for their lives as 400,000 tons (360,000 t) of mud and rocks rushed down. Ray could hear the roar of the mud as he ran. Out of the corner of one eye, he saw that the river of mud was carrying a house and a trailer. And it was catching up with him.

Ray dove between two parked cars just as the mud and wreckage slopped down. His quick thinking saved him.

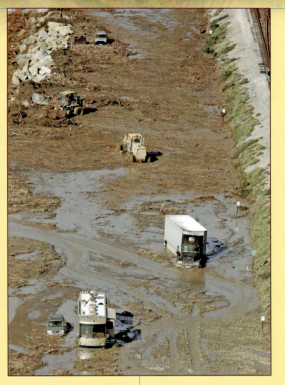

Wet, thick mud trapped trucks along Highway 101, a major freeway near La Conchita.

Morgan and Alvis were not so lucky. Both men died when the mudflow pulled them under.

Resident Jimmie Wallet's wife and three daughters died because there was no warning. "They never had a chance to get out," said Scott Hall, a firefighter who was at the disaster. "It appeared they were sitting on a couch unaware of the slide."

Mud 30 feet (9 m) deep buried part of La Conchita. It killed 10 people and seriously injured 8 others. The mudflow destroyed about 13 houses. Some were carried away and stacked up, one against another. More than 20 other homes were badly damaged.

> *I thought I was going to die buried alive.... The house started collapsing on me. ...I could feel the boards and the rocks and everything pushing me.*
>
> —Diane Hart, describing the 2005 mudflow in La Conchita, California

49

The Future

WE HAVE LEARNED LESSONS FROM PAST MUDFLOWS AND LANDSLIDES. THOSE LESSONS WILL MAKE LIFE SAFER FOR PEOPLE IN THE FUTURE. MANY PEOPLE WHO HAVE DIED IN MUDFLOWS AND LANDSLIDES COULD HAVE BEEN SAVED. THEY JUST NEEDED A WARNING THAT THE MUD WAS ON ITS WAY.

Safety was just a few minutes' walk away for many of the 23,000 people who died in mudflows from the Nevado del Ruiz volcano in 1985. What if sirens had warned them? The mud flowed in a fairly narrow path through the town of Armero. People could have walked a short distance to safety. Instead, the mud swallowed them alive.

LISTENING FOR MUD

Scientists have invented warning systems for mudflows and avalanches. Acoustic flow monitors (AFMs) are used in mudflow warning systems. These devices measure sounds that occur in the ground as mud flows. They also can estimate (guess) the size of the flow.

When AFMs detect a mudflow, they send a signal to a control center. The center then alerts fire departments, police, and other emergency workers. Warnings go out by radio, television, and the Internet.

This acoustic flow monitor keeps an ear out for mud flowing in Hoala, Hawaii.

AFM systems already have been installed on a few volcanoes where mudflows pose a great danger. Mount Saint Helens and Mount Rainier in Washington State and the Hoala Volcano in Hawaii have these systems. Scientists plan to put AFMs and other warning systems in more places where mudflows and landslides are a danger.

A bulldozer repairs damage from a
2006 landslide in Provo, Utah.

MORE AND BETTER WARNINGS

In the future, more people in these danger zones will know how to use the warnings. Communities will have evacuation plans that tell people what to do and where to go when a disaster threatens.

Future warning systems also will be more accurate. All too often, warning devices give false alarms. They sometimes send warnings when there is no real danger.

False alarms can be dangerous. People may be injured or killed as they rush to evacuate a danger zone. And what happens if there are too many false alarms? People may ignore the warning when a real disaster is on the way.

OPEN *YOUR* EYES!

Scientists and emergency workers are looking for better ways to make people aware of the risk of disasters. Telling people about the risk is especially important for mudflows and landslides. That's because these disasters often happen again and again in the same places.

People living near Turtle Mountain before the 1903 disaster knew that landslides often happened there. Nevertheless, they stayed. People are still living there.

Why do people keep living in disaster zones? Why do they build new homes, schools, and stores in places that are disasters waiting to happen? Getting people to live in safer areas could mean a future in which fewer people are hurt by landslides and mudflows.

BETTER EYES IN THE SKY

Scientists are building better cameras and other instruments that will detect landslides and mudflows from satellites in space. These instruments will map landslide and mudflow danger zones all over Earth.

This sign in southwestern Germany warns people that landslides can happen in the area.

Mud and debris swirl around a building at the foot of El Salvador's Ilamatepec Volcano. About 10,000 Salvadorans lived near the volcano when it erupted in 2005.

Cameras that provide sharper pictures are important. They will allow scientists to make better maps of areas where disasters have happened in the past. People who live in these areas then will know that they face a similar danger.

Other instruments may allow scientists to watch for tiny movements in mountains and hills. If a hillside slides 1 inch (2.5 cm) today and 1 foot (0.3 m) tomorrow, it may be getting ready for a disastrous landslide.

REDUCING THE DANGER

Such information will help people reduce the damage from mudflows and landslides in the future. People can move away from danger zones. They can install warning systems, plant trees on slopes to hold the soil in place, and plan for evacuations.

Mudflows and landslides are dangerous. But they also are rare. They happen mainly in places near mountains, hills, or high piles of soil or other material. With better warnings and information on mudflow and landslide safety, most people can avoid these disasters.

Cracks in the ground near the city of Skopje, Macedonia, where a landslide happened in 2006

PREPARING FOR LANDSLIDES AND MUDFLOWS

Landslides and mudflows usually strike with little or no warning. It is important to know the danger signs and what to do to protect yourself and your family. Warning signs can include:

- New cracks or unusual bulges in the ground, street, or sidewalks

- Sudden tilting of trees, fences, telephone poles, or street signs

- Doors or windows that stick for the first time

If a mudflow or landslide is on the way, you may hear a rumbling or rushing sound. You may see a river of mud or tumbling rock and soil. If you do, remember to:

- Run to the side, in a direction away from the danger.

- If possible, head for a hill or other high ground. Try to find shelter, such as a group of trees or a strong building.

- If you cannot escape a landslide, curl into a tight ball and protect your head.

- If you are caught in a mudflow, grab a tree or other object that is being carried along.

After a mudflow or landslide:

- Stay away from the area. More mud or rocks may be on the way. Wait until emergency officials say it is safe to return.

- Don't go into damaged buildings. They may fall down and trap you. Cracks in a chimney or foundation can mean a house is badly damaged.

- Stay away from electric power lines and telephone lines that may have fallen down. The electricity could hurt you.

Timeline

A.D. 79 Mud from the eruption of Mount Vesuvius *(right)* in modern-day Italy buries the city of Herculaneum.

1806 Part of Rossberg Peak in Switzerland collapses and kills 500 people.

1853 A landslide on Turtle Mountain, Alberta, Canada, kills 100 people.

1877 One mudflow in Ecuador travels more than 192 miles (320 km).

1881 A mountaintop near Elm, Switzerland, weakened by slate mining, collapses. More than 10 million cubic yards (7.6 million cubic m) of rock hurtles down the mountain and devastates the towns below.

1903 Coal mining weakens Turtle Mountain in Alberta, Canada, and 90 million tons (82 million t) of rock cascade on the town of Frank. The landslide kills at least 70 people.

1920 An earthquake causes a huge landslide in Gansu Province, China, killing approximately 180,000 people.

1958 A landslide in Lituya Bay, Alaska, generates a tsunami wave 50 feet (15 m) high.

1963 A landslide into the Vaiont Dam in Belluno, Italy, causes a huge wave 328 feet (100 m) high to wash over the dam and kill 3,000 people in the village of Longarone.

1964 44,000 people are left homeless after a landslide destroys bridges and homes in Niigata, Japan.

1966 A slag pile (unwanted rock from coal mines) in Aberfan, Wales *(left)*, collapses and slams into a school.

1970 A magnitude 7.9 earthquake in the central mountains of Peru creates a landslide that kills approximately 66,000 people.

1971 A 66-foot-high (20 m) river of mud buries the town of Saint-Jean-Vianney in Canada.

1972 Floods in Japan cause a landslide that kills 370 people and causes a $472 million loss in crops and homes.

1980 Mount Saint Helens erupts and destroys more than 230 square miles (600 sq. km) of land.

1983 The most expensive landslide in the United States buries Thistle, Utah. The damage totals approximately $500 million.

1985 23,000 people are killed when mud from the slopes of the Nevado del Ruiz Volcano buries the town of Armero, Colombia *(right)*.

1998 Deforestation in the Himalaya mountains and torrential rains are blamed for a massive landslide in India.

2000 A rain-soaked mountain of garbage crashes into makeshift housing in Quezon City, the Philippines. More than 100 people are killed.

2002 A landslide that was 20 miles (30 km) long fills the Karmadon Gorge *(below)* with rock and mud. The disaster completely covers the village of Nizhny Karmadon in southern Russia.

2004 The island of Hispaniola is devastated by flooding as high as 15 feet (4.6 m) that sends rivers of mud down to the villages below.

2005 Mudflows in Mexico and Central America, caused by Hurricane Stan, kill at least 750 people, injure hundreds of others, and destroy the homes where about 100,000 people live.

2006 Heavy rains and a minor earthquake cause a series of deadly mudflows in Southern Leyte Province in the Philippines.

Glossary

ash: tiny bits of rock that come out of a volcano

creep: a very slow movement of the ground

deforestation: cutting down all the trees and other plants in an area

evacuate: to leave for a safer place

friction: the force that makes it harder for one object to slide against another

geologists: scientists who study how Earth formed, what our planet is like, and how it is changing

hurricane: a huge storm with strong, swirling winds that produces heavy rain

inertia: the tendency of still objects to stay still and of objects in motion to stay in motion

lahar: a mudflow that occurs on a volcano

landslide: a mass of soil and rock that breaks loose from a hill or mountain and slides down

mudflow: wet earth that flows like a river down the sides of a mountain or hill

slump: soil, rock, or other material that drops downward a short distance onto flat land, then piles up and stops

suffocate: die from lack of air to breathe

tsunami: a wave produced by earth movement, a volcano, or a landslide

volcano: an opening in Earth's surface that sometimes erupts

Places to Visit

Frank Slide Interpretive Center—Alberta, Canada
http://www.frankslide.com/home.html
The Frank Slide Interpretive Center provides an entire town as the memorial to the 1903 landslide that claimed 90 lives. You can walk the pathways around the center to see the actual Frank Slide site.

John Day Fossil Beds National Monument—Kimberly, Oregon
http://www.nps.gov/joda/
Make sure to visit the Clarno Unit of the park. There you will see the Palisades, a cliff formed millions of years ago by lahars.

Lassen Volcanic National Park—near Mineral, California
http://www.lassen.volcanic.national-park.com/
Lassen Volcano is an active volcano. Tour the Hot Rocks area, and see where mudflows changed the landscape.

Mount Saint Helens—Washington State
http://www.fs.fed.us/gpnf/mshnvm/
Visit Mount Saint Helens, and see the results of the volcanic eruption and landslides.

Valdez Museum—Valdez, Alaska

http://www.valdez-alaska.com/valdez-museum.htm
The Valdez Museum has exhibits on the 1964
earthquake that led to a huge landslide. The landslide then caused a tsunami that traveled across
the Pacific Ocean to Hilo, Hawaii.

Vermillion Cliffs National Monument—Northern
Arizona

http://arizona.sierraclub.org/monuments/
vermilion/vermilion.html
See examples of various types of land movements, including slumps, earth flows, and slides.

Source Notes

4   Juan Tacaxoy, quoted in Karin Gezelius Bergstresser,
     "Santiago Atitlan, October 5, 2005 Mudslide,"
     Santiago Atitlan, n.d., http://www.santiagoatitlan.com/
     disaster/disaster1e.html (October 17, 2006).

4   Dr. Francisco Mendes Beauc, quoted in Laura
     Smith-Spark, "Buried Alive in a River of Mud,"
     BBC News, October 10, 2005, http://news
     .bbc.co.uk/go/pr/fr/-/1/hi/americas/4326650.stm
     (October 10, 2005).

5   Alexander Flores, quoted in "Rescuers Struggle in
     Wake of Stan," *BBC News*, October 6, 2005,
     http://news.bbc.co.uk/go/pr/fr/-/1/hi/world/
     americas/4314088.stm (October 10, 2005).

5   Diego Esquina, quoted in "Guatemala Villages
     'Mass Graves,'" *BBC News*, October 10, 2005,
     http://news.bbc.co.uk/go/pr/fr/-/1/hi/world/
     americas/4324038.stm (November 27, 2005).

5   Alexander Flores, quoted in "Flooding, Landslide
     Kill Scores," *Taipei Times*, October 7, 2005,
     http://www.taipeitimes.com/News/world/archives/
     2005/10/07/2003274789 (October 17, 2006).

13   Pliny the Younger, quoted in "Mount Vesuvius,"
     Classroom of the Future, http://www.cet.edu/ete/
     modules/volcanoes/vmtvesuvius.html (October
     17, 2006).

13   Ibid.

13   Ibid.

16   Tom Horning, quoted in Jen Shaffer, "The
     Science of Slides: A Primer on How Debris
     Flows Work," *Wildfire News*, http://www
     .wildfirenews.com/ forests/forest/analysis.html
     (December 3, 2005).

16–17 Rab Nawaz, quoted in "Survivors Ponder Life
     without Livelihoods," *BBC News*, October 29,
     2005, http://news.bbc.co.uk/2/hi/south
     _asia/4385216.stm (October 17, 2006).

20   Nelda Taglo, quoted in Angela Pagano,
     "'Promised Land' Garbage Landslide Kills at
     Least 200 in the Philippines," *World Socialist
     Web Site*, July 21, 2000, http://www
     .wsws.org/articles/2000/jul2000/phil-j21
     _prn.shtml (November 19, 2005).

21   Francesco Amato, quoted in Vania Grandi,
     "Body Search Continues in Muddy Central
     Italy," *Laredo Morning Times*, May 8, 1998,
     http://www.lmtonline.com/news/archive/
     050898/pagea13.pdf (October 16, 2006).

22   Jessie Byran Leitch, quoted in "Frank Slide,"
     Winnipeg Free Press, October 15, 1950,
     http://www.shirley.collongridge.com/
     FrankSlide02.htm (November 27, 2005).

23   Ibid.

28 Dave Crockett, quoted in Jason Manning, "22. Mount St. Helens," *The Eighties Club*, n.d., http://eightiesclub.tripod.com/id308.htm (October 17, 2006).

28 Janet Hicks, quoted in Sally Ousley, "Eruption Survivors Excited, Nervous," *Daily News*, October 1, 2004, http://www.tdn.com/helens/noFlash/mainpage.php?p=1114797670&w=P (October 17, 2006).

29 Keith Stoffel, quoted in "Debris Avalanche," *USGS*, March 19, 2002, http://pubs.usgs.gov/gip/msh//debris.html (October 17, 2006).

29 Ibid.

38 Jose Luis Restrepo, quoted in Dr. Vic Camp, "Nevado del Ruiz (1985)," *How Volcanoes Work*, October 10, 2000, http://www.geology.sdsu.edu/how_volcanoes_work/Nevado.html (November 19, 2005).

38 Ibid.

39 Modesto Bocanegra Menesses, quoted in Tomas Guillen, "A Volcano's Toll: Disaster in Colombia," *Reporter*, n.d., http://fac-staff.seattleu.edu/tomasg/web/reporter/volcano.html (November 19, 2005).

39 Alba Maria Triviedo, quoted in Tomas Guillen, "A Volcano's Toll: Disaster in Colombia," *Reporter*, n.d., http://fac-staff.seattleu.edu/tomasg/web/reporter/volcano.html (November 19, 2005).

39 Jose Luis Restrepo.

40 Civil defense official, quoted in Reuters, "Rescuers Dig for Landslide Victims," *Chicago Tribune*, September 29, 1987.

42 Diego Esquina, quoted in Frank Jack Daniel, "Guatemalan Village Turns into 'Cemetery' under Mud," *Globeandmail.com*, October 10, 2005, http://www.theglobeandmail.com/servlet/story/LAC.20051010.GUATEMALA10/ (October 10, 2005).

47 Celia Huerto, quoted in Mona Laczo, "Philippines Struggles with Storm Damage," *BBC News*, December 7, 2004, http://news.bbc.co.uk/2/hi/asia-pacific/4074859.stm (October 18, 2006).

48 Greg Ray, quoted in Robert Jablon, "Mudslide Survivor Recalls Horror," *SouthCoastToday.com*, January 14, 2005, http://www.southcoasttoday.com/daily/01-05/01-14-05/a10lo518.htm (November 17, 2005).

48 Gisela Woggon, quoted in "Southland's Record Rainfall," *Los Angeles Times*, January 12, 2005.

49 Greg Ray.

49 Scott Hall, quoted in "Hunt for Mudslide Survivors Ends," *CBS News*, January 13, 2005, http://www.cbsnews.com/stories/2005/01/14/national/main666949.shtml (October 7, 2005).

49 Diane Hart, quoted in "Hunt for Mudslide Survivors Ends," *CBS News*, January 13, 2005, http://www.cbsnews.com/stories/2005/01/14/national/main666949.shtml (October 7, 2005).

Selected Bibliography

American National Red Cross. "Volcano." *American Red Cross*. N.d. http://www.redcross.org/services/disaster/0,1082,0_593_,00.html (October 11, 2006).

Bruce, Victoria. *No Apparent Danger: The True Story of Volcanic Disaster at Galeras and Nevado del Ruiz*. New York: HarperCollins, 2001.

College of the Siskiyous. "Mudflows of Mount Shasta." *Mount Shasta*. N.d. http://www.siskiyous.edu/shasta/env/glacial/mud.htm (October 11, 2006).

Davis, Lee. *Natural Disasters*. New York: Facts on File, 2002.

Engelbert, Phillis. *Dangerous Planet: The Science of Natural Disasters*. Detroit: UXL, 2001.

Federal Emergency Management Agency. "Landslide and Debris Flow (Mudslide)." *FEMA*. March 29, 2006. http://www.fema.gov/hazard/landslide/index.shtm (October 11, 2006).

Gregory, Kenneth John, ed. *The Earth's Natural Forces*. New York: Oxford University Press, 1990.

Hancock, Paul L., and Brian J. Skinner, eds. *Oxford Companion to the Earth*. New York: Oxford University Press, 2000.

Reice, Seth. R. *The Silver Lining: The Benefits of Natural Disasters*. Princeton, NJ: Princeton University Press, 2001.

Spignesi, Stephen J. *The 100 Greatest Disasters of All Time*. New York: Kensington Publishing Corp., 2002.

U.S. Department of the Interior. "Deadly Lahars from Nevado del Ruiz, Colombia." *U.S. Geological Survey*. September 30, 1999. http://volcanoes.usgs.gov/Hazards/What/Lahars/RuizLahars.html (October 11, 2006).

———. "FAQs (Frequently Asked Questions)." *U.S. Geological Survey*. November 2, 2005. http://landslides.usgs.gov/learningeducation/faq.php (October 11, 2006).

———. "Mudflows, Debris Flows, and Lahars." *U.S. Geological Survey*. March 3, 2006. http://vulcan.wr.usgs.gov/Glossary/Lahars/framework.html (October 11, 2006).

Wheeling Jesuit University. "Mount Ranier." *Classroom of the Future*. November 10, 2004. http://www.cotf.edu/ete/modules/volcanoes/mountrainier.html (October 11, 2006).

Zeilinga de Boer, Jelle, and Donald Theodore Sanders. *Earthquakes in Human History: The Far Reaching Effects of Seismic Disruptions*. Princeton, NJ: Princeton University Press, 2005.

Further Resources

BOOKS

Allaby, Michael. *Biomes of the World*. Vol. 5, *Mountains*. Danbury, CT: Grolier Education, 1999. Michael Allaby explains the causes of landslides.

Barnard, Bryn. *Dangerous Planet: Natural Disasters That Changed History*. New York: Crown Publishers, 2003. Natural disasters have played major parts in shaping the history of the world. Barnard explains that global warming may cause more natural disasters.

Colson, Mary. *Crumbling Earth: Erosion and Landslides*. Chicago: Raintree, 2004. This easy-to-understand title explains the various types of erosion of the soil and has many helpful photographs.

Cosgrove, Brian. *Eyewitness: Weather*. New York: Dorling Kindersley, 2004. An informative book about weather and the instruments that have been used to predict and measure weather.

Goodwin, Peter. *Landslides, Slumps, and Creep*. New York: Franklin Watts, 1997. Peter Goodwin explains landslides, avalanches, and mudflows.

Newson, Lesley. *Devastation: The World's Worst Natural Disasters*. New York: DK Publishing, 1998. This book contains images of some of the natural disasters that strike Earth.

Sandler, Martin. *America's Great Disasters*. New York: HarperCollins, 2003. Sandler writes about the eruption of Mount Saint Helens and the mudflows and landslides that followed the eruption.

Vogel, Carole Garbury. *Nature's Fury: Eyewitness Reports of Natural Disaster*. New York: Scholastic, 2000. Thirteen natural disasters are examined in this book.

Winner, Cherie. *Erosion*. Minneapolis: Carolrhoda Books, 1999. The author explains how the erosion of soil causes changes in the land.

Woods, Michael, and Mary B. Woods. *Earthquakes*. Minneapolis: Lerner Publications Company, 2007. This book describes earthquake disasters, many of which caused landslides.

———. *Volcanoes*. Minneapolis: Lerner Publications Company, 2007. Learn about a variety of volcano disasters.

WEBSITES AND FILMS

Association of American State Geologists

http://www.stategeologists.org
Do you want information on landslide or mudflow dangers near your home? Check out your state Geological Survey site.

Kid's Cosmos

http://www.kidscosmos.org/kid-stuff/kids
-volcanoes-st-helens.html
Kid's Cosmos has a section on the eruption of Mount Saint Helens and the resulting mudflows.

Things to Know: Volcanoes

http://www.fema.gov/kids/knw_vol.htm
This site has safety tips from the Federal Emergency Management Agency.

All About Soil. DVD and VHS. Wynnewood, PA: Schlessinger, 2005.
Find out how erosion contributes to the formation of soil.

Erosion. DVD and VHS. Burbank, CA: Walt Disney Home Video, 2004.
Join Bill Nye, the Science Guy, in this video about the forces of erosion.

Erosion: Landslide. VHS. Bethesda, MD: Discovery Channel, 2000.
Explore the causes of fast-moving landslides!

Forces of Nature. DVD and VHS. Washington, DC: National Geographic, 2004.
The National Geographic society has produced a film explaining the incredible forces of nature that affect the world.

Thunder on the Mountain: Landslides and Avalanches. VHS. Washington, DC: National Geographic, 1999.
National Geographic brings actual footage of a quiet mountaintop becoming a raging landslide!

Index

Photo Acknowledgments

The images in this book are used with the permission of: © Anatoly Maltsev/epa/Corbis, pp. 1, 57 (bottom); PhotoDisc Royalty Free by Getty Images, p. 1 (background), all borders; © Getty Images, pp. 3, 4, 5, 7, 15, 34, 35, 37, 41, 45, 47, 53, 54, 55, 56 (bottom); © E.R. Degginger/Photo Researchers, Inc., p. 6; © AGRfoto/Alex Rowbotham/Alamy, p. 8; © Reuters/CORBIS, p. 9; © Brian Cassey, p. 10; © Tom Myers/Photo Researchers, Inc., p. 11; © Mimmo Jodice/CORBIS, p. 12; © Atlantide Phototravel/Corbis, p. 13; © Picture Contact/Alamy, p. 17; © Daniel and Flossie White/Alamy, p. 18; © W.K. Fletcher/Photo Researchers, Inc., p. 19; AP Images/Pat Roque, p. 20; AP Images/Franco Castano, p. 21; Geological Survey of Canada/Library and Archives Canada/PA-045469, p. 22; George S. Rice/Library and Archives Canada/PA-045408, p. 23; Photograph courtesy of Utah Geological Survey, p. 24; U.S. Geological Survey/photo by Lyn Topinka, p. 25; U.S. Geological Survey/photo by Tom Casadevall, p. 28; U.S. Geological Survey/photo by Dan Dzurisin, p. 29; George S. Rice/Library and Archives Canada/PA-045409, p. 31; AP Images/Kevork Djansezian, pp. 33, 48, 49; © CORBIS, p. 36; AP Images/Paul Benoit, p. 38; AP Images/Carlos Gonzalez, p. 39; AP Images/Reed Saxon, p. 43; U.S. Geological Survey/photo by Tom Hale, p. 50; AP Images/George Frey, p. 51; © DEPLiX/Alamy, p. 52; Library of Congress (LC-DIG-ppmsc-06584), p. 56 (top); AP Images, p. 57 (top).

Front Cover: © Steven Georges/Press-Telegram/Corbis; PhotoDisc Royalty Free by Getty Images, background. Back Cover: PhotoDisc Royalty Free by Getty Images.

About the Authors

Michael Woods is a science and medical journalist in Washington, D.C., who has won many national writing awards. Mary B. Woods is a school librarian. Their past books include the eight-volume Ancient Technology series. The Woods have four children. When not writing, reading, or enjoying their grandchildren, the Woods travel to gather material for future books.